# What is
# JANNAH?

## Salmah Umm Zainab

GOODWORD

We begin in the name of **ALLAH**

Most Gracious

Most Merciful

*Bismillahir Rahmanir Raheem*

Did you ever hear of a special place called Jannah?

Jannah is the Arabic word for Paradise or Garden

Does your family have a garden?

Have you ever visited a big beautiful garden or gone to a really great park to play?

What are some of the things you like best about gardens and parks?

Do you remember reading about the first man and woman Adam and Eve?

**ALLAH** ~glorfied and exalted is He~ put Adam and Eve in a beautiful Garden after giving them life.

He made them healthy and strong and wonderful to look upon.

He gave them everything they could ever want.

They were never too hot or too cold.

Their clothes were made of shining light.

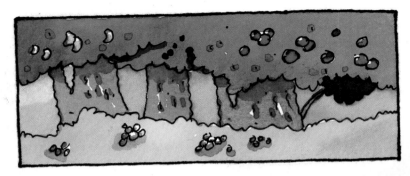

In their Garden were fruit trees and nut trees,

bushes and vines, foods of all kinds,

the clearest water and sweetest milk,

fragrant, colorful flowers,

amazing creatures on land and water, birds large and small and many things to explore and discover.

The Angels asked
**ALLAH**
~glorified and exalted is He~

why He would create beings who could do terrible things upon the Earth? The Angels could do no wrong,

6

and Jinns, even though they had free will and could choose to do wrong, were not creatures of earth but of fire.

ALLAH reminded the Angels that He knows what they do not know. Everything that happens, good or bad, is part of His greater plan.

ALLAH ~glorified and exalted is He~ has told us through Prophet Muhammad ~peace and blessings of Allah be upon him~ that everyone who does their very best

8

to obey **ALLAH** will have the chance to live forever in **JANNAH** after **ALLAH** brings all things to an end on the Last Day and then creates them again.

**ALLAH** ~glorified and exalted is He~ tells us about **JANNAH** in the Glorious **QUR'AN**

For the righteous are Gardens in nearness to their Lord, with rivers flowing beneath; therein is their eternal home; with companions pure (and holy); and the good pleasure of Allah. For in Allah's sight are (all) His servants
— *Quran 3:15*

How long can we have a home in Jannah?

Be quick in the race for forgiveness from your Lord, and for a Garden whose width is that (of the whole) of the heavens and of the earth, prepared for the righteous. —*Qur'an 3:133*

How big is Jannah?

Their Lord doth give them glad tidings of a Mercy from Himself, of His good pleasure, and of gardens for them, wherein are delights that endure: They will dwell therein for ever. Verily in Allah's presence is a reward, the greatest (of all). —*Qur'an 9:21, 22*

What is the greatest thing about Jannah?

Allah hath promised to Believers, men and women, gardens under which rivers flow, to dwell therein, and beautiful mansions in gardens of everlasting bliss. But the greatest bliss is the good pleasure of Allah: that is the supreme felicity. —*Qur'an 9:72*

What kind of home can you have in Jannah?

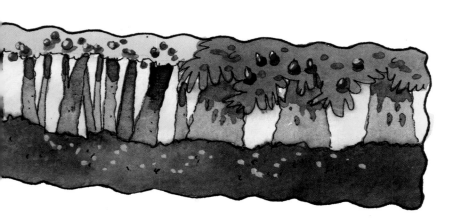

Those who believe, and work righteousness,
- their Lord will guide them because of their faith:
beneath them will flow rivers in gardens of bliss.
(This will be) their cry therein: "Glory to Thee, O Allah!"

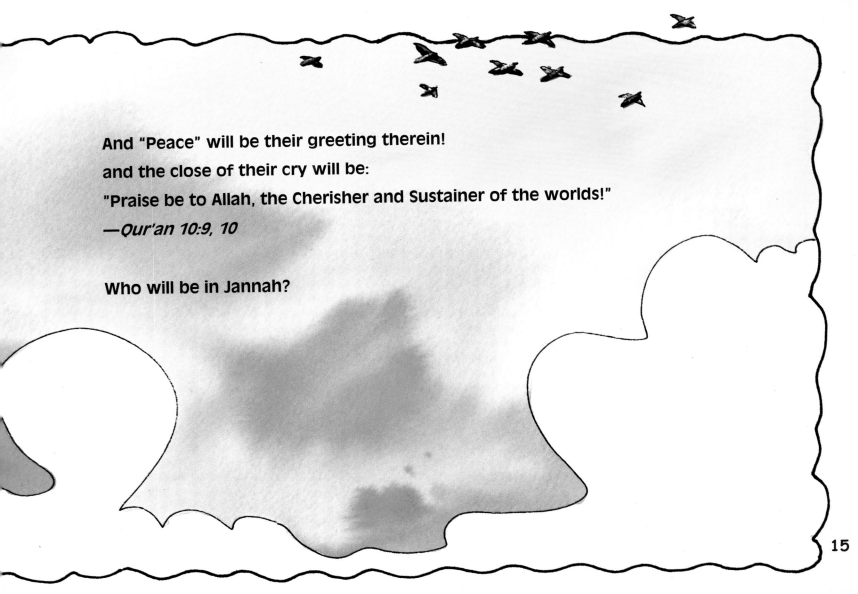

And "Peace" will be their greeting therein!
and the close of their cry will be:
"Praise be to Allah, the Cherisher and Sustainer of the worlds!"
—*Qur'an 10:9, 10*

Who will be in Jannah?

The righteous (will be) amid gardens and fountains (of clear-flowing water). (Their greeting will be): "Enter ye here in peace and security." And We shall remove from their hearts any lurking sense of injury: (they will be) brothers (joyfully) facing each other on thrones (of dignity). —*Qur'an 15:45-47*

What will happen to the hurt we felt in this world?

For them will be Gardens of Eternity; beneath them rivers will flow; they will be adorned therein with bracelets of gold, and they will wear green garments of fine silk and heavy brocade: They will recline therein on raised thrones. How good the recompense! How beautiful a couch to recline on! —*Qur'an 18:31*

What can you wear in Jannah?

"For them there will be therein all that they wish for: they will dwell (there) for aye: A promise to be prayed for from thy Lord." —*Qur'an 25:16*

What would you wish for?

Gardens of Eternity will they enter: therein will they be adorned with bracelets of gold and pearls; and their garments there will be of silk. And they will say: Praise be to Allah, Who has removed from us (all) sorrow: for our Lord is indeed Oft-Forgiving Ready to appreciate (service): —*Qur'an 35:33*

To whom will we give all our thanks and praise in Jannah?

21

He will forgive you your sins, and admit you to Gardens beneath which Rivers flow, and to beautiful mansions in Gardens of Eternity: that is indeed the Supreme Achievement. —*Qur'an 61:12*

What is the Supreme Achievement?

But Allah will deliver them from the evil of that Day, and will shed over them a Light of Beauty and (blissful) Joy. And because they were patient and constant, He will reward them with a Garden and (garments of) silk. Reclining in the (Garden) on raised thrones, they will see there neither schorching heat nor biting cold.
—Qur'an 76:11-13

Will there be anything unpleasant in Jannah?

## Remember...

What is Jannah?

Would you like to live in Jannah forever?  Why?

What do you think is the best thing about Jannah?

What else would you like to have in Jannah?

Who would you like to have with you in Jannah?

How can you get to Jannah?